THE VERY

Best

of

You

LIFESTYLE COLLECTION SERIES

James Frederick Jones

ISBN 979-8-89309-517-3 (Paperback)
ISBN 979-8-89309-518-0 (Digital)

All scripture referenced is taken from the
Holy Bible using various translations

Covenant Books
11661 Hwy 707
Murrells Inlet, SC 29576
www.covenantbooks.com

To my wife, Kim T. Jones, who I am honored and blessed to have in my life, yesterday, today, and forevermore.

To my children, who continue to touch my life in such a precious way:

My daughter Jasmine and her family, my son-in-law Marc Fauntleroy, and their daughters, Blake and Drew.

My daughter Jené and her family, my son-in-law Kevin Freeman, and their daughters, Avery and Kyla, and son, Kevin Jr.

And my son, James F. Jones Jr.

To my mother, Mary, a.k.a. Betty, and sisters Angenean and Deanna, along with my entire family and extended family, to God be the glory for the things He has done.

Last but not least, to my mother-in-law Barbara Thorne and godmother Dorothy Cannon, I am forever grateful and thankful for you both.

CONTENTS

Acknowledgments vii

Introduction: Giving It All You Got ix

Good Courage: Be Strong and Courageous 1

Setting Goals: Vision Is Required 4

Change Method: Formality of Alteration...................6

Love Supreme: Highest Quality..............................8

Created Force: In His Image and Likeness................10

Humbly Submitted: Adding Value 12

The Art of Perfection: Something to Behold...............15

Don't Give Up: You Got This...................................17

Knowing When to Pivot: The Right Moves................20

Mental and Spiritual Health: Becoming Whole............23

Next Level: Newness and Progression 25

Last Things: All You Can Ask or Think 27

Hit the Reset: A Requirement Necessary 30

All Things: Immense without Limits........................32

Uncharted Waters: Let It Flow................................35

Prayer of Hope: Hold Unswerving 38

Prayer of Peace: The Lord Provides 41

Prayer of Love: Show Me the Way 43

Be Fruitful and Multiply: Follow the Plan 45

Brilliance Awakening: Every Step You Take 48

The Main Thing: Be You..51

Blueprint: Pay It Forward 53

ACKNOWLEDGMENTS

In loving memory of my beloved
brother, Billy L. Jones
(1972–2020)

A very special thank-you to these ministry leaders who have provided me with spiritual guidance and leadership over the years: the late deacon Melvin Ross, the late reverend Tony James, the late reverend Dr. Bernard F. Alston, the late reverend Dr. Hoarce W. Sheppard Sr., and the late reverend Dr. Howard O. Jameson. In addition, thank you as well to Rev. Dr. Byron Jameson, and Rev. Dr. Kenneth J. Caldwell.

To my church family Dare 2 Imagine and Pastor Rev. Dr. Kevin R. Johnson, we continue to imagine greatly because only the best will come from it, and that makes life better.

Giving It All You Got

The Lifestyle Collection Series is about the spiritual journey to everyday living. The moral standards to living a productive life involve taking action upon which principles can be built. An understanding of a principle such as this is a guiding sense of requirements and obligation of right conduct, an adopted rule of method for your life application. There is a biblical principle that states, "Wisdom is the principal thing; therefore, get wisdom, and with all thy getting, get understanding." The amount of knowledge, intelligence, insight, and wisdom comes from God and God alone; so as you desire more of Him, the very best will come of it, bringing out the best in you and in your life to come.

Whenever you purpose in your heart and mind to be the best of yourself, it will bring about a change and quality of life as you adhere to every moment. There is nothing more profound than giving life all you have to the fullest, desiring the best version of yourself every day. The best of you identifies being in the moment and living life with the best intentions, producing confidence, faith, and trust, which are the subjects of truth and divine decree. You are the product of God's creation, and God has equipped you to prosper in every area of your life. As you approach life with the best attitude, good things will come your way. In all that you do in life, strive to be the best at it and allow God to add the rest in you only like He can.

Each chapter of this book is like short story lessons filled with heartfelt messages designed for you to explore and manifest the beauty of God's glory and image, which is to become of you as you give life all that you must give.

As an author, creating a collection series geared to a specific lifestyle of living is what I am excited about sharing. It is my hope that you will enjoy reading these chapters just as much as I enjoyed writing them for you. As a cancer survivor, I humbly rejoice in the fact that God is using such words to be a blessing to you and others. God's truth matters and remains to be the force and spirit of these words centered on creating a way and lifestyle to behold.

May God give you heaven's dew and earth's richness.

Be Strong and Courageous

*Be strong and courageous, do not be afraid;
do not be discouraged, for the Lord your
God will be with you wherever you go.*

It takes courage to succeed in life. Having an ability to exert a greater strength within yourself physically and mentally is what good courage looks like. Courage is spirit-driven. There was a song written some years ago by the Gospel recording group the Winans, titled "Wherever I Go" ("Wherever I go, let your spirit follow me"). If there is anything you need more than life itself, it is the spirit of God covering you. Courage is that which you possess; it is the quality of mind or spirit that enables you to face difficulty, danger, pain—without fear, but with bravery.

The strength of your courage lies in its ability to help you overcome. You can perceive courage as an essential quality of life because it runs deep and is rooted within your soul and stands alone. The magnificent behavior of courage does not waver at all, but it is steadfast and firm in its position, which identifies the character and nature of good courage and hope. A vital part of everyday life and living is the conquest of hope. Hope is the feeling that gives you courage that what is wanted can be had or that events in your life will turn out favorable for you. Your ability to act on what you believe becomes a testament to your faith. Everyone has been given a measure of faith, but it is how you apply it that brings your best results.

The best from you is with good intention, and your greatest potential is believing you have what it takes. One of the most profound truths is this: "All things are possible to them that believe." Good courage propels you to be an achiever, and if you do that in good faith, you are doing it right.

Here is what I have come to realize about good courage: it will not falter when you understand it. Courage is a gift, and "all good and perfect gifts come from God the Father." There is a standard of living and behavior that God desires for you to have and good courage is a part of it. "God is no respecter of persons" and will give you every opportunity in life to prevail. God's promises are a declaration of His expression toward you with an assurance for a lifetime. With God, it is with the sense of knowing that greater things are coming. The best leverage you can give to yourself is opening up to God and incorporating His spirit in all that you do. God can do for you that which is impossible for you to do without Him. Whatever the narrative is in your life always, let the goodness of God be all the courage you need every day without fail.

Vision Is Required

There is no vision, the people perish.

One who is willing to set goals will have a life of promise and purpose. Whenever you plan to succeed, you can achieve remarkable things. Goals, which are the results or achievement toward which effort is directed, prepare you for success. A goal-oriented individual is one with a vision and a plan that sets them apart and keeps them moving onward.

There are many things in life that are important, but how you see it matters the most. Getting the best results from your life requires a plan of action. Your best days can become the ones that you planned. One of the most remarkable things about setting goals is forward-thinking. Someone who thinks carefully considers what is important to them with a clear and defined understanding. Clarity gives you the ability to think with a sound mind of acumen, balance, comprehension, and intelligence.

Setting goals enhances your opportunities for success in life, and preparation is a key element. When you are prepared, it allows you to maximize your ability, efforts, and potential. A great complement and component to setting goals is having passion, a strong amorous feeling of affection to pursuing goals that complement your desires and what you want to accomplish out of life.

There can be many distractors when setting goals, but you must acquire good regimens and habits that produce, develop, and keep you progressing along the way. Always imagine with an expectation of reaching your goals for better things ahead.

"Many are the plans in a person's heart, but it is the Lord's purpose that prevails." God gives you all that you need to be the best in life. God's plan for your life is always sure and one on which you can depend. You may not always understand how God is moving on your behalf, but know that it is for your good. If you trust God's process for your life, then the goals you set for yourself will come in alignment with what God has for you. God's promises are true, "and God is able to make all grace abound to you, so that in all things, at all times, having all you need, you will abound in every good work."

Let setting goals be a motivation and indication of what you expect from yourself. All that you are and ever hope to be is in your determination to see it through. Be reasonable and diligent at every aspect of your goal-setting because only then will it become attainable to the plan.

Formality of Alteration

*To everything there is a season, a time
for every purpose under heaven.*

As time is of the essence, so is change. Each season of your life is something that changes over time. Change is sure to occur, happen, or come to you at some point. The act of changing or fact of being changed is the formality of alteration in nature and content. How you comprehend change is transformation and modification of your expression. It is through the transition to change and the way you perceive it that can work best for you.

What change differentiates is your vulnerability to accept something new. The method of change is action-oriented, an element that deals with your heart, mind, and soul. Your willingness to evaluate an unfamiliar perspective, discover and perceive innovative ideas and concepts, shows your ability to grow yourself even more. You can be inspired through change and come away with a whole new meaning and outlook on life when open to it.

The method of change evaluates your understanding and beliefs and causes you to examine yourself from the inside out. Change is a decision that must be embraced and exerted. Although people often resist change because of their own fears, change can be good for you if you allow it. Change challenges every aspect of your emotions and involves taking some risk; but it can benefit you in accordance with what is good, proper, and just, when at the right time and place.

Apart from all life's complexities is learning when and how to adapt to change. Anything that is worth changing always justifies the change that is needed. Whenever you measure the quality or value the effect of a change, you discover the condition that is granted. The condition of a change method is with respect to each situation and circumstance that has presented itself to be changed.

When your attitude is right, your altitude is even greater for something new. God always spoke from the parable of doing something new. "Behold, I will do a new thing." Your new is in your response to receive what God is doing and saying to bring about a change in areas of your life. An intricate part of God's process for your life is changing the outcome. If you say that something has changed or that it has affected you beyond measure, you are emphasizing that it has primarily done this. Everything that God changes in your life is for your good, and His methods are sure and everlasting to no end.

Highest Quality

The first and greatest commandment is love.

Love is a treasure and a true matter of the heart. *Love* is the most powerful word created from God; and the substance that comes from it is pure. American saxophonist John Coltrane declares in the liner notes of his 1957 recording of "A Love Supreme" that he had this spiritual awakening, and this recording of this song was a thank-you to God as a means and privilege to make others happy through music.

"Love Supreme" is that kind of love that is of the highest degree or quality of life. Love is what love does; it leaves an impression on you. The authority of love is superior to all others. God intended for love to bring out the best in you as you gravitated toward it. What is true of love is that it is a profoundly tender and enthusiastic affection for another. It has been written that God so loved the world (us) that He gave of Himself (His Son), that you would come into the knowledge of His love.

The created force behind all humanity is God's love for you. Love is universal, and God's love is sovereign to say the least. What is so supreme of God's love is that it is heartfelt and of the highest magnitude paramount to its devotion. There is no greater love than the love that God has for you. One of the best things you can do in life is to pay love forward. Love is gentle yet fierce, which anchors your gratitude. A part of being the best is showing God's love coming from you. When you love God first, it is easier to love others. Why God first? Love is not love if it is not from the perfection of God's love. God defines love and represents the best of what love must give. God's love is consistent and never fails. When you are not given the best of your love, you diminish the value of what God intended for love to look like coming from you.

True love is from a place of your heart and always thinking of others more than itself. "For out of the abundance of the heart the mouth speaks." The best of you always comes from the goodness of your heart and is regarded as precious and beloved. Love who you are and be happy about it, not selfishly or out of vain deceit but rather as a supreme inspiration of beauty to behold.

In His Image and Likeness

In the beginning God created the heaven and earth.

You were created in the image and likeness of Almighty God. God is the source and power of life, which defines all humanity. The creating force of God that is within you is the act of producing or causing you to exist; it is the fact of you being created. The best in you and from you is an attribute of the created force of God's spirit at work in you. The true character and quintessence of your creation and creativity is in your willingness to pursue it.

As you press toward the mark of being the best version of yourself, you will reach your goals in life when you keep God at the forefront of it all. Allowing God to navigate your life transcends you beyond every imaginable circumstance or situation you will ever have to face in life. There is nothing you cannot conquer with God on your side. God is the only one who can help you become all that He created you to be. Being diligent, devoted, and dedicated serves well in your creative ability to be the best. There is nothing wrong with wanting to be the best, so do not think it strange because it is a part of what God desires of you to become.

Self-image is an important process to your creativity. "And have put on the new [spiritual] self who is being continually renewed in true knowledge in the image of Him who created the new self." The physical nature of who you are, and the attributes thereof, are best lived when combining a spiritual approach to life. When you approach something, you get closer to it. You are a spirit-being experiencing life through the lens of human nature.

The created force of energy behind you is that of spirit, soul, and body to bring out the best in you and what you have to offer. You are important to God and a special gift He created to make an impact. When you are making an impact on others, it shows that you care about making a difference. Do not settle for any sort of mediocrity in life but strive to become a force to be reckoned with. This is the likeness of who you are, giving your best and when you do, others take notice.

As life continues to unfold and evolve for you, take the time to enjoy and cherish each moment that life brings toward you. The created force that you are is well on its way to greater things ahead.

Adding Value

Be completely humble and gentle; be patient,
bearing with one another in love.

Humility is the way to God's blessings.

Humility can become one of your best and most effective traits and characteristics. Humility is the quality or condition of being humble. To the humble, God gives patience, peace, and gentleness. Becoming humble adds value to you as a person and as a quality of life for you. However, it takes a lot of work from you and a submitted heart to be and remain humble. Have you ever been around someone and they are just too full of themselves? Make sure that does not become you. Let humility speak well of you in every situation and circumstance.

There is a fine line between confidence and arrogance, and that is humility. Humility breathes confidence, but arrogance breathes cockiness. Humility is a way that leads to a great stature. God shows favor to the humble, but pride closes the door to spiritual growth. It is through humility that God opens the door of your life to more of His grace upon your life. Practice humility often because it will go a long way for you and create the best results in your life. Humility will take you as far as you allow it to.

> Do nothing out of selfish ambition or vain conceit; rather, in humility value others above yourselves.

> When pride comes then comes disgrace, but with humility comes wisdom.

> Humble yourselves before the Lord, and He will lift you up.

> Live in harmony with one another, do not be proud but be willing to associate with people of low position; do not be conceited.

Learned behavior is best lived when you put it into a course of action. Treat others the way you want to be treated, and in doing so, you take thought for what is right and gracious and proper in the sight of everyone. The good of you will always come forth when you submit to doing good. Being the best is about becoming skillful in the gifts and talents that God has given to you. So many times, the word *becoming* is used and taken lightly, but it is in the humble submission of you and your desire to become all that God has for you to be. In all your endeavors, seek to master your gifts and talents, allowing God to lead the way and see the best of you prevail greatly.

Something to Behold

*But let patience have its perfect work, that you
may be perfect and complete, lacking nothing.*

It has been said that beauty is in the eye of the
beholder—as with art and its expression of explicit detail
to perfection.

The highest degree of proficiency, skill, or excellence is
perfection. The art of perfection is an art form that is a creative space of self-expression. A formal analysis of a work
of art describes how the elements and principles of artwork
go together. Bringing out the best of you requires diligence,
which shapes and molds you to who you can become.

A key and principle element to your perfection is
having patience—a quiet, steady perseverance with diligence. Allowing patience to attach itself to you develops
your growth and perfects who you are. It is through perfection and dedication that great habits become a part of

you. Great habits are those tangibles you practice, drill, and rehearse to bring out the best in all that you do.

The art of your imagination is what propels your perfection and fuses the flames of greatness inside of you. Your ability to elevate to another level as you discover more about yourself is a fundamental principle to your perfection. What manifests your perfection is your desire to be great and the arduous work to becoming your own masterpiece.

"You are God's workmanship," the beautiful art of His perfection and accomplishment. God's perfect plan for you is something that is for your well-being, and "God will perfect that which concerns you." Do not be moved by any of your flaws because everyone has them; no one is perfect. God knows exactly what you need and how to get the best from you.

What matters most in your perfection is having God's hands upon it. "Like clay in the hand of the potter," so are you in the hand of God. God provides all the guidance and insight you need to perfect every part of you in every way. Opinions of life come and go, but what you establish becomes your own.

Make what you become your standard of excellence; in other words, the means in which you live, becomes the art of your perfection to who you are. Life always finds a way of showing you the beauty of God's perfection when you seek it out. Quest to discover the very best of what God has for you, and in doing so, He will turn your imperfections into a beauty of art.

DON'T GIVE UP

You Got This

*Let us not become weary in doing good,
for at the proper time we will reap a
harvest if we do not give up.*

Whatever you do in life, do it whole-heartedly, with the utmost sincerity, enthusiasm, and commitment.

I have adapted this saying that the greater the commitment from you, the more is required of you. God has blessed you with a life of His good gifts that they would shine through you greatly. "Every good and perfect gift is from above." The gift of life is about not giving up but perfecting the good of God in every way, bringing out the best in you. God has an invested interest in all that you desire to accomplish, and "where God guides, He provides."

Life can be treacherous at times, but never is it the plan of God for you to give up. What God is looking for is your trust in Him to see you through your life's journey. God wants you to come away knowing that He is all you need.

> His divine power has given us everything we need for a godly life through our knowledge of Him who called us by His own glory and goodness.
> For this very reason, make every effort to add to your faith goodness; and to goodness, knowledge; and to knowledge, self-control; and to self-control, perseverance; and to perseverance, godliness; and to godliness, mutual affection; and to mutual affection, love.

Do not give up on loving yourself and the life that comes with it. The power of your perseverance through love will always bring out the best in you every time. God is more than able and more than enough as you emerge in the life that He has set before you.

As life goes, it is filled with many seasons, and each period and condition is based on the plan of God. To become seasoned and mature in life, you must learn how to be strong in grace. Your grace is your manifestation of God's unmerited favor operating in your life. To value life is to endure the process, because in doing so, you come to respect all that you have to give into.

> Give, and it will be given to you.
> A good measure, pressed down, shaken
> together, and running over, will be poured
> into your lap. For with the measure you
> use, it will be measured to you.

God did not bring you this far in life for you not to see greater promises. God is faithful to fulfill all His promises toward you. Stay true to who God has created you to be and don't give up.

The Right Moves

This is the Lord's doing; it is marvelous in our eyes.

Every little thing in life matters;
it is the grand scheme of living.

The cycle of life is going to happen; it repeats itself at some point, but how you pivot makes all the difference. Pivoting is a sudden shift or turning point that is crucial to your life story. To pivot is to recognize the need to make an adjustment. The necessity of pivoting is to maintain forward progress. Pivot is all about instinct—a natural intuitive tendency to act. Life can change without warning, and knowing what to do next is of the most extreme importance.

The crossroads of life are those pivotal times of knowing. "Stop at the crossroads and look around you. Ask for the ancient paths, where the good way is, and walk in it.

You will find rest for your souls." When you pivot in the right direction, it becomes a pinpoint of reference for you. Your every move in life should be intentional; although you may have a limited perspective of what that is, God already knows what is best for you. God wants your life to overflow with mercy, love, and compassion.

Knowing when to pivot is relying on God to position you where you need to be. Life is filled with roadblocks, obstruction, and barriers, but God knows the way in which you should take. You should never feel stuck in life, because that is a clear sign that you need to pivot. Being stuck is being out of position, and that is not the plan of God for your life.

> "For I know the plans and thoughts that I have for you," says the Lord, "plans for peace and well-being and not for disaster."

It is noticeably clear that God wants to see you progressing in life.

Therefore, when you feel that impulse and inclination or you can see that you need to pivot, doing it God's way is going to bring forth all you need in that moment and time. God can enlighten your thoughts and abilities in a way that will lead you in the right path. When you pivot in life, you want to have that assurance that you are making the correct choice for yourself. Knowing what you ought to do is a constant reminder that you need God's help.

God provides for you a level of confidence like no other. If there is something magical that confidence does, it is that it gives you that feeling and belief of trusting yourself more than anything else. Whenever you feel you are at a loss to know what to do next, try pivoting your way to God for your best results.

Becoming Whole

*Beloved, I pray that in every way you may succeed
and prosper and be in good health physically,
just as I know your soul prospers spiritually.*

Taking care of your well-being is your responsibility. Wellness is the complete integration of body, mind, and spirit. The realization that everything you do, think, feel, and believe influences your well-being. When you become influenced, it affects your actions, behavior, opinions, among other things. "Whatever things are true, noble, just, pure, lovely, of good report; if there is any virtue and if there is anything praiseworthy meditate on these things." To bring out the best in you is finding the good in your mental and spiritual capacity. Every part of your health is about having a sense of peace within. It is the peace of God that brings about peace of mind and heart and gets you through the anxieties of life. Peace allows you to function at your highest level mentally and spiritually. "The Lord gives strength to his people; the Lord blesses his people with peace."

Mental and spiritual health is about becoming whole. Whole, referring to a thing that is complete in itself—nothing missing, broken, or lacking in its mental or spiritual state of being. There is nothing more that God wants than to see you completely whole in spirit, soul, and body. When you function at a level of wholeness, the very best of you is being displayed. The beacon of light that you are shines ever brightly when your mental and spiritual health is in a good place; and when it is not, you do not function at the best of your ability. Your capacity to do your best is when you are feeling your best. Do not allow anything or anyone to disrupt, discourage, or control your mental and spiritual health—because it can become a detriment to you, only if you allow it to. You must take responsibility and complete control of your life every day; then you will see the good results from your choice to live healthy mentally and spiritually. Often there are those who do not feel the need to discuss mental and spiritual health, but it is a silent killer in so many ways. The devastation and impact of something that causes you to live unhappily need to be dealt with. Any form of sadness and depression is unhealthy and can spiral out of control, but God is able to make amends from it all. Life is choice-driven, so choose to live a healthy life and enjoy the gift of living above and not beneath, because you deserve it.

Newness and Progression

*But they that wait upon the Lord shall renew
their strength; they shall mount up with
wings as eagles; they shall run, and not be
weary; and they shall walk, and not faint.*

A place of jubilee is where I long to be.

When one speaks of Next Level, it means a significantly more advanced, better, or more extreme space that you occupy. From a spiritual perspective and space, Next Level is a place of destination for your mind, spirit, and body— to experience the supernatural power of God. The very best of you have been tested and tried on every level. "But He knows the way that I take; when He has tested me, I will come forth as gold." Gold represents something refined, precious, beautiful, noble at heart; and that is the very best of you. Next Level is the awareness that something greater is before you and awaiting for you to level up. Life is about preparation and getting you to experience something new. Your new can be that of something refreshing. You say that something is refreshing when it is pleasantly different from what you have been experiencing. When you are refreshed, you feel restored and renewed with a vitality of energy to elevate to another level. That which is designed to move you more than anything in life is the spirit of God at work in you. "God is working in you, giving you the desire and the power to do what pleases Him." You are God's spirit in the earth that He takes good pleasure in, according to His will and purpose for your life. Your next level of living should be something desirable and worth looking forward to bringing about a newness and progression in your life for you to experience. It has been said that experience is life's best teacher, and God is at every moment of it. God is always there in your life to get you to that next level. The journey of your pathway in life is always connected to your level of understanding and to your next steps to take.

> So be content with who you are, and
> don't put on airs. God's strong hand is on
> you; He'll promote you at the right time.
> Live carefree before God; He is most care-
> ful with you.

When you have put in the excellent work that it takes to better yourself, it always brings about a greater return and motivates you to operate on new levels, while the elevation of your journey continues.

All You Can Ask or Think

*I know that there is nothing better for people than
to be happy and to do good while they live.*

*Your last chapter in life should
be your most fulfilled.*

Living is a state of being, and the period and times of your life have been well documented along the way. The conclusion of the matter has been the evolution of your life's journey.

*Just as you can see your own face
reflected in water, so your heart reflects
the kind of person you are.*

At the end of each day, it is all about the impact and impression that life holds on you. Everything you do in life takes on a shape of its own. When you are more aligned with your purpose, life feels certain and meaningful. Your life is your legacy, and God will complete the story of it all. You can take comfort knowing that God has the final say in matters that concern you. Whatever you do in life, cherish every moment, because it is all you have. It is not always how you start out in life that counts the most, but how you finish to bring about the best outcome for you.

The race is not given to the swift or
to the strong but to the one who endures
to the end.

The only way to make sense of the last things is to realize that God is the sustainer and provider to all things. Nothing happens in life except through God and by His will. You owe it to yourself to know God like no other. Do not settle through someone else's opinion about God but come to know God for yourself.

This is how we know that we live in
Him and He in us; He has given us of His
spirit.

The spirit of God is ever present to lead and guide you to be the best version of yourself. It is the spirit of God that is the giver of life and identifies with who you are. Take notice of the last things you think of because the next thing you do reflects that emotion and reaction. And finally, you should abound increasingly in the life that God has blessed you with. Life is a privilege and a gift that only God can provide. The greatness of who you are is in the invisible power of God's glory.

> Now to Him who is able to carry
> out His purpose and do superabundantly
> more than all that we dare ask or think
> infinitely beyond our greatest prayers,
> hopes, or dreams, according to His power
> that is at work within us.

Let your *last things* become even greater than the former things, because of what God has done forever and more in you to bring out the best of you and forevermore.

A Requirement Necessary

The Lord is my shepherd.

You already have everything you need.

A need is a requirement, necessary duty, or obligation wanted or deemed to have. The urgency and attention it takes for you to conquer your journey in life is ever before you. There are times in life that you will feel burnout, or it is like you just keep running into a wall, but know that there are brighter days ahead. The cares of this world can take a toll on you, but do not worry because God has it all in control concerning you.

A shepherd is one who watches, guards, and protects his own day and night. You are never out of the safety or reach of God's provision. God will go through the extreme for you because He cares for you that much. God is the very thing you need in your life to sustain you and help you hit the reset to life. There is this saying referred to as Monday mantra, known as a means to reset, refocus, and restart. You can even refer to this notion as a reboot to your day and fresh start. Hitting the reset to life is something that is warranted and helps you realign your priorities, because the intricacies of life can get away from you at times and require taking new thought and action. To worry or fret in such matters does not change a thing in your life, but God can. It is God who will reset and restore you to your happy place. God is the true source of happiness, strength, hope, and wisdom; and those who are in His favor will always have these blessings. Having the favor of God on your life is what helps you hit the reset button. The goodwill of God provides you with everything you need, desire, or even want out of life.

A good hitter in baseball misses and gets strikes at times, but what makes them the best at what they do is how they make their adjustments to reset, to make the hit. This is just like God, who knows exactly what you need and how to get the best from you, because He is your shepherd who will make sure that you have everything you need to be the best. There is a verse in Psalm 23 that depicts God so well as it relates to you hitting the reset: "Even if I walk through a valley as dark as the grave, I will not be afraid of any danger, because you (God) are with me." Hitting the reset button in life is a viable part of your growth and maturity as you manifest in the life that God has given you to best represent yourself, until the day of His coming.

Immense without Limits

*I can do all this through Him
who gives me strength.*

Just do it.

The incredibly famous tagline Just Do It from Nike's founder Phil Knight has developed into an inspiration to many. To be inspired is to be imbued with the spirit to do something. You can even go on to say that being inspired is that of a supernatural or divine influence resulting in you being equipped and able to do *all things*. God's ability is immense, to say the least, to bring about the best results in your life. In a world where all things can be considered, it is God who has given you the power to choose and do the right things according to His will. God's will in your life is apparent, as He provides everything you need; and the joyful content, He gives you. There is nothing greater than having God in your life to make life better.

His divine power has granted to us (all
things) that pertain to life and godliness.

To be wise is to live in godliness, reflecting the nature of God during your everyday life. How you become the best version of yourself is not just addressing some of the things in your life that you may have to suffer at times, but looking to God in (all things) of your life.

I know whom I believed and am con-
vinced that He is able to guard what I have
entrusted Him until that day.

There is nothing that God is not able to do through you because of the power of His spirit that is ever present to you. Wherever you are in your life, God is there with you for your good. The goodness of God is what makes life worth living because it is not temporary but ongoing to the core of who God is. There is this saying that God is good all the time, and all the time God is good; and this is ever so true because He has been just that good to you. In knowing this, you should strive to be a good example of all the good that He extends toward you every day. God always acts in a way that is true, noble, right, and good because it reflects who He is—always and in all things. Making life meaning-ful and relatable is what gives your life value and purpose. Every chance you get in life, you should take on a "just do it" mentality because it is a direct reflection of what God is able to do in you and through you. Take confidence in knowing that you have what it takes to be the best at whatever you put in your heart, mind, body, and soul to do.

Let It Flow

Draw nigh to God and He will draw nigh to you.

Let it flow.

The river of life is one that can flow as a constant stream of everlasting water to no end. The same can be said about life in general because it is always flowing as well. Life moves in a way that is uncharted; it is unknown until you explore the depth of it. One of the greatest attributes that God has given you is the ability to have insight and gain intuitive understanding and discernment. To be familiar with something is to have a sense of knowing or being well acquainted; but in the instances of uncharted waters, this is not the consensus at all.

Uncharted waters are like the unfamiliar areas of your life that make you feel inadequate and uncomfortable. It is not until you draw nearer and closer to God that He puts your uncharted waters into perspective. God brings a level of consistency and a continuous flow to your life that is uncanny to anything else that is around you. Everything that is out of reach for you, God can bring it right to where you are at any moment and time. Uncharted waters are just another way to get God's best from you. There is absolutely nothing you need to fear or even be afraid of when God is near and dear to you. The truth to the matter is when you are faced with uncharted waters in your life, you are exactly where God wants you to be because it is there where you can experience a deeper level of living.

> Blessed is the one who finds wisdom,
> and the one who gets understanding.

You should live life in a way that challenges you to be all that you can be. It is not until you come to a place of uncharted waters that you are challenged to step out into the deep. The deeper you exercise your faith in God, the more of Himself He will reveal to you. It is that faith which helps you move uncharted waters out of your way; because when things in your life are flowing in the right direction, you can reflect so much better in those moments of uncertainty.

> You will be like a well-watered gar-
> den, like a spring whose waters never fail.

God can always justify the places and things that He sets before you, especially the things that are unknown to you without His understanding. Do not let uncharted waters keep you from your next blessing; know that God is always there to get you over to the other side.

Hold Unswerving

That which was from the beginning, which we have heard, which we have seen with our eyes, which we have looked upon and our hands have handled of the Word of life.

Let us hold unswervingly to the hope we profess, for He who promised is faithful.

All glory, honor, and praise be to You, Lord, who is sovereign and has all power and authority in heaven and earth. I humbly submit myself to the Spirit of Your presence that I might receive the hope of Your glory and promise.

Now hope does not disappoint, because the love of God has been poured out in our hearts by the Holy Spirit who was given to us.

No matter how things may look in my life at times, my hope will remain in You alone. My time here on earth is only for a moment, and I am hopeful for better days ahead. With a heart of thanksgiving and expectations, my hope is centered on the fact that when I pray, You never cease to amaze me.

> Many, O Lord my God, are the wonders which you have done, and your thoughts toward us; there is none to compare with You. If I would declare and speak of them, they would be too numerous to count.

Awesome are You, God, in all Your ways, and You are worthy to be praised. When I take a close look at the life You have given me, I am so blessed and eternally grateful. I would not change a thing as I reverence in the hope of who You are. Holy are You, Lord God Almighty, and I declare the victory You have predestined for me through faith, love, and hope.

> Faith is the substance of things hoped for.
> Love never fails.
> And hope makes us not ashamed.
> May the God of hope fill me with all joy and peace in believing, so that by the power of the Holy Spirit I may abound in hope.

This is my earnest prayer and petition from my heart: that all things will work out for my good, in the name of the Father and of the Son and of the Holy Spirit. Amen.

The Lord Provides

*The Lord gives strength to his people, and
the Lord blesses his people with peace.*

Most gracious, holy, and wise God, I magnify Your name in all the earth as I speak Your peace over my life today, declaring it through the freedom You have granted me.

The earth is the Lord's and the fulness
thereof; the world, and they that dwell
therein.

I proclaim Your peace around me in a world that is full of problems, difficulty, issues, worry, disorder, and unrest, but because of You, Lord, will I not lie in distress. I rejoice in knowing that Your peace gives me comfort, energy, and balance that will stand the test of times, as it has been proven repeatedly. Prayer is what gives me peace of mind.

> You will keep in perfect peace those
> whose minds are steadfast, because they
> trust in You.

Having a calmness of inner peace is my heart's desire as I rely on Your mercy and grace that You have set before me today. Righteous are You, "and the effect of righteousness will be peace, and the result of righteousness, quietness and trust forever." My confidence is in You, "Wonderful Counselor, Mighty God, Eternal Father, Prince of Peace," all day long. I can be assured and rest in knowing that Your peace for me is everlasting to no end. Lord, You promised rest of love, healing, security, and above all, peace of God and peace with God. Nothing else in this world compares to You and the peace I get from You through the power of prayer. "To the only wise God our Savior, be glory and majesty, dominion and power, both now and ever." Amen.

Show Me the Way

*Bless the Lord, O my soul, and all that
is within me, bless His holy name.*

For the Lord is good and His love endures forever.

The affection that I have for You is that of deep gratitude and tenderness toward Your loving kindness. I will seek the intimacy of You, "because Your love is better than life, I will praise You as long as I live. I will lift up my hands in prayer to Your name." Prayer is my love language, and, Lord, as You abide in me and I in You, You will remain my lifeline.

Show me Your ways, O Lord; teach me Your paths.

My love will reflect that of who You are to me. Your love is powerful, never ceases, never changes, and never fails. When nothing of us could help, it was Your love that lifted me.

> You have granted me life and stead-
> fast love, and your care has preserved my
> spirit.

I will speak boldly of this because You have captured me and continue to set me free in loving others as I should. May I manifest the image of You through the love that You so generously give and have shown me. Just like the dew that falls from the heavens and declares Your glory, let Your love forever reign over me for a lifetime. My commitment is to love more and to love better. "Do to others what you would have them do to you." Everything that I am and ever hope to be is connected to the love You have shown and given me repeatedly. This is my sincere prayer as I continue to trust and believe in You, forever and a long time, for that's how long I'll love You. Amen.

Follow the Plan

*I am the vine; you are the branches. If you remain
in me and I in you, you will bear much fruit.*

His way is perfected.

Whenever you consider the things of God first as your plan, only good can come from it. Being the best version of yourself is likened to firing on all cylinders. By way of explanation, operating at the most desirable or greatest level of efficiency and productivity in your life. A plan is not a plan if it has not been thoroughly thought out, and what God has prepared for you is going to change the whole landscape of your life. Life as God intended is for you to function at your fullest capacity as the human branch designed to derive all its life substance from the vine. The function of the vine is to pump life to the branches, and the function of the branch is to produce the fruit of the vine. God has a plan for your life, and it will produce a harvest for you.

> "So also, will be the word that I speak,
> it will not fail to do what I plan for it; it
> will do everything I send it to do" to bring
> out the absolute best of you.

It has always been God's plan for you to be fruitful and multiply. When something is fruitful, it produces good and useful results; just to add when things are multiplying, it brings about increase and favor into your life. "Blessed be the Lord, who daily loads us with benefits." It has always been God's plan for you to rely on Him for your well-being. Just like a vine, God helps you develop and grow into what He has purposed for your life. For anything to be fruitful, it must identify with a seed, which causes a branch to sprout up, to produce fruit from the vine. You are a spiritual seed that God has created in the earth to have dominion and power, blossoming and flourishing into something beautiful. How you multiply as a fruit from the vine is by being a strong branch, that God can trust and depend on as His creation.

> If you abide in Me, and My words
> abide in you, you will ask what you desire,
> and it shall be done for you.

When God blesses you to multiply, He increases you in many ways that you would affect others through what

He has done through you. God did not just create you to live and have immense success, but He has also blessed you with the ability to help others share in the same experiences of His blessings. What God wants more than anything is for this world to be full of people who share His own image: "And have put on the new {spiritual} self who is being continually renewed in true knowledge in the image of Him who created the new self."

Every Step You Take

Out of darkness the light shall shine.

Stay woke.

For God, who said, "Let brilliant light shine out of darkness," is the one who has cascaded his light into us—the brilliant dawning light of the glorious knowledge of God, who is awakening us to let our light shine. Coming into most situations, you are usually a little in the dark until you can decipher for yourself the whole matter at hand. More than anything else, God values who you are long before anyone else recognizes your brilliance. From the void of darkness to the light of His creation, God has spoken and awakened the heaven and earth of His goodness. God's goodness represents everything that God is and everything that He has for you to experience from Him. To be awakened is a recognition, realization, or coming into awareness of something to uncover. God's presence comes with heaven's brilliance to bring out the very best of you.

> As for me, I will behold thy face in
> righteousness, I shall be satisfied when I
> awake with thy likeness.

When God awakens your spirit of understanding, He gives you complete contentment, perfect knowledge, everlasting rest, ineffable peace, and communion with Him, which brings about rapturous joy to your life. God's intentions for you are to be filled with His light.

> And this is the message we have heard
> from Him and announce to you, that God
> is light and in Him there is no darkness at
> all.

Recording artist Debby Boone recorded a beautiful song some years ago that spoke the sentiments of God's light; it was titled "You Light Up My Life": "You gave me hope to carry on, you light up my days and fill my nights with song." Even through the shadow of darkness, you can find your way to the light because your brilliance is in the light you carry. One of the greatest gifts that God has given you is His word. "Your word is a lamp to my feet and a light to my path." God's word is like sunshine that illuminates everything around you to be awakened—to lead and guide you through the pathways of life that He has set before you. Every step you take in life is one that is of the most importance to God as He delights in every detail of your life. Even in the darkest of times, God will always come through to bring about His desire. God's greatest desire is for you to choose Him in love as He has chosen you. "In the same way, let your light shine before others, that they may see your good deeds and glorify your Father in heaven."

THE MAIN THING

Be You

Whatever you do, do all to the glory of God.

Be the best example you can.

Out of all the stories ever told, the Bible is the one with the greatest examples. What is so intriguing about stories in the Bible is that they do not stand alone, but they give the best examples for you to examine yourself. We all could use a little self-examination in our lives because it gives us that awareness that is so much needed in our lives to survive.

In the New Testament of the Bible, the word *glory* is often used to describe the activity of people as they give praise and honor to God. In appreciating God throughout your life, the best you can do is remember to keep the main thing the main thing: giving God all the glory and honor He so deserves. "His glorious name deserves praise forevermore."

When author Stephen Covey coined the phrase "keep the main thing the main thing," its focus and efforts were on keeping what you do as an example that you live by. Your life always reflects what is important to you and has a staple on how you live. Having a lifestyle that keeps God as the main thing deserves much praise. "For God will reward each of us according to what we have done." The inspiration behind God being the main thing in your life is His presence. "Seek the Lord and His strength; seek His presence continually." God's presence is the epitome of heaven on earth. Simply put, God's eminent and great merit is what separates Him from everything else that life holds.

Looking at all the things you must juggle in your life from time to time, it is so good to know that you can always count on God in all times of need. The best thing about having God as your main thing is His ability to make you a fitting example. God will personally fashion you according to His love and wisdom. "Whoever is wise will observe these things, and they will understand the lovingkindness of the Lord." The meaning and observation here is that God is worthy of your confidence and love. What God does is help you see the bigger picture of a thing that is Him. "For in Him we live and move and exist."

This is what God does: He advocates for you to be the very best of yourself through Him as a living example of His glory. God's constant provisions are what enable you to have the ability to keep the main thing the main thing in your life.

Pay It Forward

*A good person leaves an inheritance
for their children's children.*

Leave no stone unturned.

Legacy, as we know it, is the impact of something left as a blueprint and a guide that others can follow. When speaking of blueprint, it is that in which a process or plan of action has been established. God wants nothing more than to establish His blueprint in you in many directions, to constantly bring out the very best in you continually. What is good is having a good quality of life, and every human being holds within them a combined heritage of characteristics that God has already given you to accomplish everything He wants out of life for you. Treasuring every good gift that God has put on the inside of you is the blessing to receiving more.

> I will give you hidden treasures, riches
> stored in secret places, so that you may
> know that I am the Lord.

What good is it to have the blessings of God and not pass it on. When you compact the fact that God's DNA is a part of your bloodline, you then begin to see the magnitude of you in establishing your own legacy and inheritance to doing something special. You are a special gift that God has gifted to be a wonderful blessing.

> And I have filled him with the spirit
> of God, with skill, ability, and knowledge
> in all kinds of crafts.

God has crafted you to be wise in every area of your life. The wiser you become, the more substance and depth you add to yourself as God's very own. There are no shortcuts in life, only the paths that lead to your legacy.

On October 26, 1967, six months before the Rev. Dr. Martin Luther King Jr. was assassinated, he spoke to a group of students at Barratt Junior High School in Philadelphia, Pennsylvania, and he asked them this question: What is your life's blueprint? He suggested some of the things that should begin your life's blueprint. Number one in your life's blueprint should be a deep belief in your own dignity, your worth, and your own "somebodiness." Don't allow anybody to make you feel that you're nobody. Always feel that you count and that your life has ultimate significance. Dr. King closed the question in which he asked them, saying you must have as the basic principle the determination to achieve excellence in all your endeavors. Therefore, continue to establish the blueprint of your life and watch what God does beyond your imagination as you become the best version of yourself.

ABOUT THE AUTHOR

James Frederick Jones is a husband, father, grandfather, father-in-law, brother, son, friend, army veteran, ordained minister, and native of Florence, South Carolina.

He is a graduate of Wilson High School in Florence. James now resides in Philadelphia, Pennsylvania, where he has lived for over forty years. His secondary education includes a bachelor and master of arts degree in theology from Jameson Christian College; his doctor of theology is from International Christian University.

What James is most proud of is his relationship with his beautiful wife, Kim T. Jones, as they were married on May 16, 1987. What is very exciting to James now these days is being a new author; he is committed to creating a lifestyle collection series that touches the heart, soul, and mind of all of us on purpose. James is thrilled to be able to minister in this way as an author as he gives all glory and honor to God for all that He has done and still doing in his life.